meeting

JESUS

2007-8 NMI
MISSION EDUCATION RESOURCES

❊ ❊ ❊

BOOKS

AFRICA'S SOUL HOPE
The AIDS Crisis and the Church
by Ellen Decker

BABOONS ON THE RUNWAY
And Other Humorous Stories from Africa
by Richard F. Zanner

MEETING JESUS
by Keith Schwanz

THE NUDGE IN MY SIDE
Stories from Indonesia and the Philippines
by The Bob McCroskeys

THEY SAW ONLY FEET
More Life Lessons from Missionary Kids
by Dean Nelson

A LOVE STORY FROM TRINIDAD
by Ruth O. Saxon

❊ ❊ ❊

ADULT MISSION EDUCATION RESOURCE BOOK

RESPONDING TO MISSION CHALLENGES
Editors: Aimee Curtis and Rosanne Bolerjack

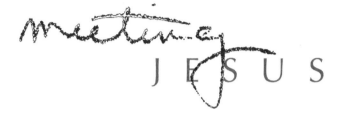

meeting
JESUS

keith schwanz

Nazarene Publishing House
Kansas City, Missouri

DEDICATION

Paul wrote, "I always pray with joy because of your partnership in the gospel" (Phil. 1:4b-5a). The *JESUS* film ministry in the Church of the Nazarene is truly a partnership. *Meeting Jesus* is dedicated to two segments of this vast partnership: the hundreds of *JESUS* film team members in every region of the world who faithfully proclaim the gospel and the Harvest Partners who support their ministry.

CONTENTS

DR. KEITH SCHWANZ is the assistant dean and lecturer in church music at Nazarene Theological Seminary (NTS). His responsibilities include serving as director of the NTS Center for Lifelong Learning, coordinating the chapel program, and directing the Seminary Singers. Prior to moving to Overland Park, Kansas, Keith served as a pastor in the Northwest.

Keith is the author of several books, including *Shouts at Sunrise: the Abduction and Rescue of Don Cox* and *Words of Life and Love: World Mission Literature Ministries*, both part of NMI book series. He served as editor of *Sainteté à l'Éternel!: chants pour le peuple de Dieu (Holiness Unto the Lord: Songs for the People of God, 2005)*, the first French hymnal produced by the Church of the Nazarene. He has written numerous articles for *Holiness Today, Herald of Holiness, Illustrated Bible Life,* and *The Preacher's Magazine.*

Keith is married to Dr. Judi Schwanz, professor of pastoral care and counseling at Nazarene Theological Seminary. Together they have taught in pastors' retreats and conferences in Mexico, the Dominican Republic, Puerto Rico, Canada, and the United States. They live in Overland Park, Kansas, and have two adult children, Karla and Jason, and one grandchild, Judah James.

ACKNOWLEDGMENTS

JESUS film team leaders and district, field, and regional *JESUS* film coordinators send reports to the JESUS Film Harvest Partners office each month. *Meeting Jesus* was written from these reports. Thanks to Brian Helstrom, Alissa Monterroso, and Gloria Wittmer at JESUS Film Harvest Partners for their help with collecting the stories and photos used in this book.

I also appreciate the guidance provided by Wes Eby, retired NMI editor, and Judi Schwanz, my wife and the first person who reviews the drafts. These two people helped ensure that what I intended to say is actually what people ended up hearing. Thank you.

ACKNOWLEDGMENTS

FOREWORD

Every week *JESUS* film teams share God's love with the lost. These workers are dauntless in their tenacity to fulfill the Great Commission. Every month our office receives the reports of their labor, and they often read like the New Testament.

In this book, Keith Schwanz has done a masterful job of weaving the two together: that which was penned in the first century and that which is being written today. It reads as one continuous story because God is still God, and He's still doing God stuff.

Jesus told His disciples they would do greater things than they saw Him do; that if they lifted Him up, people would be drawn to Him; and they would build His Church and the gates of hell would not prevail against it. The *JESUS* film teams witness to these truths as they respond with unreserved obedience.

The harvest is ready. It is coming in, and it is bountiful. The *JESUS* film ministry is a part of that harvest. Working cooperatively with denominational ministries and other Kingdom entities creates a synergy that has great impact. God is truly doing a mighty work.

This book is an accurate portrayal of the ongoing work of Jesus Christ around the world. I invite you to digest its words and realize one more time with certainty that what Jesus said is true: You are on the winning team. Satan continues to be defeated. The church of Jesus Christ is being built, and it is all being done to please the Father. God gets all the glory!

Thank you for partnering in the harvest.

You are loved,

Brian Helstrom
Missionary, Church of the Nazarene
Assigned as Executive Director,
JESUS Film Harvest Partners

INTRODUCTION

God has transformed millions of people through the *JESUS* film ministry. Since the formation of the partnership in 1997 between the Church of the Nazarene and Campus Crusade for Christ, the producer of the *JESUS* film, hundreds of Nazarene teams have shown the film thousands of times to millions of people who have made a decision for Christ.

As this book goes to print, the *JESUS* film is available in over 979 languages. This causes many viewers to stand in wonder when they hear Jesus speak in their native tongue. As they watch the film, they identify so strongly that they feel like Jesus has physically come to their village to proclaim the Good News, heal the sick, and teach the things of God. Some viewers marvel at Jesus' compassion and immediately abandon a lifestyle marred by abusive behavior. Others observe the miracle of healing, then ask the *JESUS* film team members to pray for their own healing. Alcoholics and drug users find liberation. Skeptics meet God. Millions of wonderstruck people encounter Jesus and are transformed.

Sometimes thousands of people see the *JESUS* film at one showing. A large-screen team projects it onto a screen made of parachute material. The image can be viewed from both sides. The audio track plays through a portable sound system. All of the equipment is powered by a generator if electricity cannot be procured from another source. In January 2004 about 40,000 people saw the *JESUS* film at one time at a soccer field in Uganda, most of them refugees from war-torn neighboring countries.

In other situations a small-screen team may introduce the *JESUS* film to one person at a time. Using a television and video player, or a personal DVD player, the evangelist and the inquirer view the film together, often in secret. Most small-screen teams operate in countries where political or religious pressure prevents public evangelistic events.

The *JESUS* film has been seen on a bus in Zambia. While traveling to their next ministry assignment, one team noticed that the bus had a built-in video player. They asked the bus driver for permission to introduce the film to the passengers. He consented. The bus passengers liked the film so much that they played it three times during the seven-and-a-half hour trip. Four passengers knowingly passed by their stop just so they could continue watching it. When the *JESUS* film team reached its destination, the bus driver urged them to go on with him to the next town. They gave him a video tape instead.

THE GOSPEL

The producers of the *JESUS* film used the Gospel of Luke as their primary source. Luke said that he "carefully investigated" the life and ministry of Jesus, then wrote an "orderly account" of what he discovered. He used personal encounters with Jesus to demonstrate the transformational power of God that attested to Jesus as Messiah.

What if Luke wrote his Gospel today and used the testimonies of people transformed while watching the *JESUS* film? That question guided the writing of this book. *Meeting Jesus* incorporates testimonies of people transformed in the 21st century, but it emulates the writing style Luke used when he told the stories of those who met Jesus in the 1st century.

Each chapter begins with a brief description of an encounter with Jesus as recorded in the Gospel of Luke and portrayed in the *JESUS* film. I present the encounter much like a storyteller would relate the story. The opening narrative ends with a quote from the Gospel of Luke, including the reference where the story can be found in the Bible.

The chapter then goes on to recount several stories of present-day encounters with Jesus because of the faithful ministry of Nazarene *JESUS* film teams. Each *JESUS* film story connects with the theme of that chapter's opening narrative. As is true for the Book of Luke, this book is the compilation of many relatively short stories. To help the flow, I have borrowed transitional phrases from Luke as the narrative moves from story to story, like "One day Jesus went to another region" and "Jesus traveled through the countryside, sharing the Good News." These phrases help smooth the transitions between stories.

Since this book is intended to read like one of the Gospels, I refer to the *JESUS* film simply as JESUS (upper case). For example, I state that JESUS goes to a village, not that a team took the *JESUS* film to the village. References to Jesus, the Man, appear in the usual form (initial capital letter). For this "gospel" the *JESUS* film teams and local church leaders are referred to as disciples.

Each chapter closes with a summary verse from Luke. I used this method and selected these particular quotes to help the reader glance beyond what can be placed on a printed page. This book contains only a few kernels of the vast harvest being reaped today.

Ultimately, *Meeting Jesus* is not a book about the *JESUS* film or the film teams or the Church of the Nazarene. It is a story of personal encounters with Jesus. The dramatic portrayal of the Savior's life, death, and resurrection in the *JESUS* film leads to a transformational encounter with Christ. Listen to the testimonies. Look at what God has done. Allow the evidence to strengthen your own conviction that Jesus is the Anointed One.

ONE

Then JESUS Came

John the Baptizer spoke strong, confrontational words that forced the people to face their need for repentance. Many people saw baptism as an insurance policy, but seemed unaware that the premium required a radical reorientation of how they lived. John insisted they consider the cost. In calling the crowd to make an abrupt turn, John told them to share with those in need. When confronting the tax collectors, he instructed them to make a fair assessment every time. Concerning the soldiers, he told them never to be guilty of extortion.

Not one to use politically correct language, John called the crowd a "brood of vipers." His words emphasized the fact that their lives were a tangled mess. He chose a graphic description—a pit of poisonous snakes.

Some heard the voice of a prophet in John's words. Could he be Messiah? Or was he the man Isaiah said would prepare the way for the Anointed One?

Others did not attribute such a lofty role to John but saw him merely as a nuisance. King Herod, for one, did

not like the rebuke he received from John. Herod impris-
oned John to take him out of circulation. The decreased
volume of the public discourse pleased Herod.

Prison life changed John. No longer an eyewitness,
John relied on visitors to describe the happenings in the
world. No longer the man with the answers, John had
many questions. Concerning the reports John heard about
Jesus' emerging ministry, John wondered if Jesus was Messiah. At Jesus' baptism, John heard the voice declaring
God's pleasure with Jesus. But now John felt uncertain. A
lot had changed for him since those heady days.

So John selected two close friends to investigate
and bring him a report. They were to go to Jesus and
ask Him straight up whether He was *the* Messiah who
the prophets said would come. The question was direct,
but Jesus answered indirectly.

He told the questioners to look, listen, and pay
attention to the evidence around them. Then He added,
"Go back and report to John what you have seen and
heard: The blind receive sight, the lame walk, those
who have leprosy are cured, the deaf hear, the dead are
raised, and the good news is preached to the poor"
(Luke 7:22b).

LOOK . . . LISTEN

Akbar worked in a factory that made bricks. His
job was to keep the place clean. Akbar attended Christian services but had not made a decision for Christ.

While he worked he often sang songs he learned at church but did not really understand. To other workers at the factory, Akbar appeared to be happy and content.

His family saw a darker side. Akbar suffered from a recurring nightmare in which he lost his sight. He often awoke crying, terrorized by the thought of being blind. His family worried about Akbar's sanity.

Lame and of limited value to the community, Yohana felt casually discarded on a trash heap.

Then Akbar heard that JESUS would be in a neighboring village. He walked three miles to get there. Akbar watched in rapt attention as blind Bartimaeus called for Jesus to touch his eyes. When Jesus healed the blind man, Akbar started shouting for Jesus to touch him too. God answered Akbar's prayer and freed him from his fears.

Yohana hated himself. No one else valued him either. Lame and of limited value to the community, Yohana felt casually discarded on a trash heap. His response to the rejection included anger directed at no one in particular but everyone in general.

Then JESUS came to his Kenyan village. Yohana watched as Jesus compassionately cared for the outcasts of society. He strongly identified with those to whom Jesus offered peace and wholeness. Yohana made a decision to follow Christ that night. He rejoiced in a Savior who loved a lame man.

Raj owned several properties, including four stores in a shopping center. Leprosy, however, overshadowed his success as a businessman. He spent a great deal of money for medical treatments, only to leave the doctor's office disappointed time after time. Believing he was incurable, Raj's family gave him some money and told him to leave. They wanted no part of his life as a leper.

Then JESUS came. When the disciples found Raj, they touched him as they prayed for him. Instead of pushing him away in fear because of his disease, they came close. The local congregation gathered around Raj to pray for his healing. Many fasted too. Within four weeks, all signs of the skin disease disappeared. Jesus healed another leper.

❊   ❊   ❊

JESUS went to a prison in Ecuador. The disciples received permission from the colonel in charge to show the film just outside the prison walls. Prisoners pushed against the fence to get a good view. Police officers stood nearby. People from the neighborhood gathered close. That night 6 people from the neighborhood, 12 prisoners, and 18 police officers made decisions for Christ. The pastor of the local Nazarene congregation formed a new "cell" group as they studied the Bible and prayed together. Jesus brought freedom to the prisoners.

In another community, the local Nazarene pastor looked on in amazement as people gathered to see JESUS. In addition to the religious restrictions in this

A large crowd gathers to watch the *JESUS* film.

closed Caribbean country, witchcraft practitioners often stifled ministry. The pastor had faced strong resistance, so to see 95 people assembled for JESUS far surpassed his expectations.

The team especially noted the presence of a 35-year-old man they met earlier. Now seated near the video projector, this man had thrown them out of his house a short time before. As was their custom, the disciples went door-to-door through the town, talking with people, giving them tracts, and inviting them to see JESUS. This man had violently rejected their invitation and driven them away. Now he sat with the others.

The disciples knew a little of his story. This man eagerly invited demons to inhabit his body. While possessed, he walked on broken glass and permitted others to cut his skin with machetes. His neighbors knew the power of darkness.

Then Jesus changed him completely. This man stood as the first of 59 people who gave themselves to God that night. Great rejoicing filled the place.

As the disciples dismantled the equipment and prepared to leave, the man approached them with a simple request. Would they go with him to help him clean house? They eagerly returned to the home where just hours before they were rejected. This time the man tossed out all of his witchcraft articles. Jesus had truly brought freedom to the captive.

"They were all filled with awe and praised God. 'A great prophet has appeared among us,' they said. 'God has come to help his people.' This news about Jesus spread throughout . . . the surrounding country" (Luke 7:16-17).

TWO

Forgiven

Simon invited Jesus to come to his house for dinner. Being a Pharisee, one of the "separated ones," Simon looked forward to talking with Jesus without the common people pushing to be near him. The seclusion of his house would provide a welcome relief from the clamor of the crowds. Simon anticipated a lively conversation on what it meant to live by the Law of Moses.

When Jesus arrived He joined Simon and a few of his friends for a meal. As was the custom, the diners reclined at the table, their heads near the table with their feet trailing away. Casual conversation enhanced the gathering as they ate.

Suddenly a weeping woman burst into the room and ran to Jesus. Simon sat speechless. The sanctity of his house had been violated by this intruder. He felt embarrassed to have his guests so inconvenienced. What kind of host would allow such a thing? When it registered what she was—a prostitute—Simon became furious with the imposition.

Jesus didn't move. The woman's tears bathed Jesus'

feet as she stood behind Him. When she noticed what she had done, she knelt down to towel them with her hair. She kissed Jesus' feet, then reached for an alabaster jar filled with sweet smelling ointment that she lovingly massaged into His skin. The perfume permeated the room.

Simon didn't like the smell of what happened. He regained his composure enough to mutter that if Jesus knew what he knew about this woman, He wouldn't let her touch Him.

Jesus understood Simon but still did not recoil from the woman's touch. Instead, He told a story about two men who took out separate loans—one for a very large amount and another one for a smaller amount. After some time the lender canceled both loans. Jesus then asked Simon which man he thought would be the most grateful.

Simon thought it might be the one who had the bigger debt.

"Then [Jesus] turned toward the woman and said to Simon, 'Do you see this woman? I came into your house. You did not give me any water for my feet, but she wet my feet with her tears and wiped them with her hair. You did not give me a kiss, but this woman, from the time I entered, has not stopped kissing my feet. You did not put oil on my head, but she has poured perfume on my feet. Therefore, I tell you, her many sins have been forgiven—for she loved much. But he who has been forgiven little loves little.'

"Jesus said to the woman, 'Your faith has saved you; go in peace'" (Luke 7:44-47, 50).

AUTHENTIC LOVE

JESUS went to a Brazilian neighborhood where many prostitutes worked. As some disciples prepared for a showing, others invited people to see JESUS. Ana received the invitation but said she could not watch the film since she needed to go to her job. She walked away.

Many people watched JESUS and responded to the invitation. As the disciples counseled those who made a decision for Christ, Ana suddenly rushed in.

"I heard JESUS while I was working. I need a Savior."

A disciple led Ana in prayer as she confessed her sins and received God's forgiveness. This woman also discipled Ana as she left her life of sin and began to walk in the glory of God's grace.

Wanting to get away from the squalor conditions, Josiane willingly went with the woman, only to be forced into prostitution.

JESUS and his disciples then traveled to Rwanda. Violence in her home country forced Josiane to escape to a refugee camp. One day a woman came to the camp to "rescue" young women. Wanting to get away from the squalor conditions, Josiane willingly went with the woman, only to be forced into prostitution.

A woman is baptized in Africa.

JESUS came to the village where Josiane now lived. On four consecutive nights she watched JESUS. At one of those showings she invited Christ into her life. Jesus pardoned her and set her free. The disciples found a family in the local church with whom she could live. Josiane learned to follow Jesus in all aspects of her life.

Disciples in Mozambique distributed a leaflet showing JESUS in one village. The tract was entitled "Jesus Forgives Sins and Transforms Sinners" and included the story of Jesus forgiving the prostitute. Three women who attended the meeting admitted that they worked as prostitutes. All three prayed, asking God to forgive them and help them leave their lives of sin.

When JESUS went to Uruguay, Hortensia cried as she told the disciples about the strife in her home. Her husband was an alcoholic and very violent. She needed help.

Hortensia invited JESUS to come to her house. After seeing JESUS, she confessed her sin and accepted Christ as her personal Savior. Hortensia's husband met Jesus too. Jesus helped him break the grip of alcohol and tobacco addictions. Liberated at last!

As the reality of the new life in Christ began to take hold of Hortensia, she found the courage to share something that brought her great shame. For years she tried to keep it hidden that she worked as a prostitute. Those in the neighborhood who knew of her life in the darkness saw the light of God's love in the way she began to live after meeting Jesus. The group of Christians that met in her home grew until they became a fully organized church.

LIFE AND DEATH

Once JESUS found a woman named Ruth. She felt a tremendous burden of guilt as she watched JESUS. When the film ended, her story came pouring out. Her husband had discovered that she was guilty of adultery and threatened to divorce her. Before he could leave, however, she poisoned him. He died, but no one ever suspected she caused his death.

Ruth came to Jesus in search of forgiveness. God answered her prayer when she asked Jesus to be her Savior and Lord.

On another day, JESUS met a man in Argentina reeling from a violent argument with his wife. Still in a simmering rage, he made plans to murder his wife and son, then commit suicide. Before he could enact his plan, however, he came upon a crowd gathered to watch JESUS. As he saw the compassion of Christ, his heart was troubled by his own hostility. No one needed to convince him of his sin; he was painfully aware of his great need.

Following the film, the man sought out a disciple with whom to talk. He admitted his murderous plan and repented of the evil in his heart. He asked God to forgive him, then sought forgiveness from his wife and son. Jesus restored the man to his family.

✳   ✳   ✳

When JESUS arrived in a certain Mexican city, shouts filled the air. About 30 police officers tried to capture members of The Vampires, a local gang. One man lost an eye in the struggle. Most of the gang got away.

Minutes later, when the disciples went to the house where they had arranged to show JESUS, they were turned away. Fear kept the owner locked inside the house. He did not want to draw attention to his family during this stressful time in the neighborhood. A

Setting up the film equipment

woman who lived three houses away saw what was going on and offered her house from which JESUS could speak.

The disciples set up chairs and the projection equipment, praying for safety while they worked. When the sound system was ready, they used it to broadcast an invitation to the people. At first no one responded because of the earlier confrontation with the police. Slowly, one by one, people began to gather to see JESUS. When a small crowd had formed they started.

Partway through the film one of The Vampires showed up. He stayed in the shadows but positioned himself so he could see JESUS. After watching a while, he sent a child to get a disciple.

"I want to talk with you," the gang member said.

The disciple responded, "Jesus loves you and wants to hear what you have to say."

"I just got out of jail. My wife has asked for a divorce and has taken our children. I don't know what it means to be happy."

The disciple noticed that other gang members had slipped in to watch JESUS too.

"My name is Victor," the man continued. "I am the leader of The Vampires. I am tired of women, alcohol, drugs, money—they are destroying me. Pray for me."

The disciple prayed with Victor and presented God's plan for salvation as they talked quietly in the shadows.

As Victor turned to walk away, he repeated his request: "Pray for me."

SAVED FROM DESTRUCTION

JESUS went on to a city where two young men plotted the murders of their neighbors. Earlier, when thugs came looking for their uncle, these neighbors provided exact information on where to find him. The young men had been raised by their uncle, and they witnessed the horror of seeing him killed. Now they wanted revenge, and the informant neighbors were their target.

They met Jesus before they could carry out their plan. On two successive evenings the men watched JESUS. He touched them with peace. "The words of Jesus when He asked for forgiveness of those who caused Him to suffer on the Cross were the words that touched our hearts," one man testified. "We couldn't stay seated at the altar call. We gave our lives to God."

✻   ✻   ✻

Now some who believed in Jesus fell away. Bako made a decision for Christ in 1992. For three years he served the Lord, then slipped back into the ways of sin. He started drinking. He stole things. The police arrested him mány times and put him in jail. Sometimes he suffered beatings in retribution for his thievery.

Even though Bako knew the evilness of stealing, he didn't seem able to control himself. Angry over his inability to stop, he became convinced that his index finger caused his unwanted behavior. One day, in desperation, he bit off his index finger in an attempt to reform. His pain only increased.

Then JESUS came to his Ethiopian village. Bako watched JESUS on three consecutive nights. At the final showing, Bako responded to the invitation and accepted Christ as his Savior. The transformation began.

Many people in the community saw a remarkable change in Bako. They knew his reputation. Some had suffered because of him. Now they wanted to know what had happened. Jesus changed the community as many others made a decision for Christ because of the dramatic difference they saw in Bako.

In another village, Kamanga lived in shame. Kamanga had stolen a neighbor's chicken. The elders in his Malawi village confronted him and ordered him to make restitution. Kamanga did so, but this action did not resolve the problem of shame. People in the village spoke poorly of him after this incident. They scorned him and his family. The weight of shame forced Kamanga to avoid as much contact with others in the village as he could. He hid from his friends.

One day Kamanga found a friend in Jesus. After he made a commitment to Christ, he publicly announced he would never steal again. Then he added, "I have the assurance that Jesus has freed me of this shame and embarrassment."

"Everyone was amazed and gave praise to God. They were filled with awe and said, 'We have seen remarkable things today'" (Luke 5:26).

THREE

The Anointed One

Many times Jesus found a private place to pray alone. Occasionally He would take the disciples with Him to the quiet place. This was one of those times.

Jesus interrupted the solemn reverie with a question for the disciples. He wanted to know who the crowds said He was.

The disciples could answer that question. They had just returned from a trip where they ministered in the same way they had seen Jesus serve. He gave them authority over demons and the power to heal. Jesus commissioned them to boldly proclaim the kingdom of God. The disciples had been with the people, so they had several answers ready. They told Him some thought He was John the Baptist raised from the dead. Others felt He was Elijah, the one promised to come back before Messiah arrives. Still others thought one of the ancient prophets had returned.

Jesus wasn't as interested in answers to the first question as He was to the answer of the next one. The first question was an ice breaker. The next question got to the core of the issue.

"Who do you say I am?" (Luke 9:20a).

To respond to this question the disciples could not skip on the surface using the stones of another's opinion. It forced them to delve deep into their own conviction.

Peter, often the first of the disciples to respond at times like this, broke the silence. Unlike other occasions when he seemed impetuous, this time Peter's response came across well-reasoned and confident.

"Peter answered, 'The Christ of God'" (Luke 9:20b).

FIRST HEARING

People in a remote village in Ecuador had never heard about Jesus. In an attempt to appease their longing for a higher power, they built a small shrine and placed several dolls inside. The people named each doll and worshiped them.

A group of 10 young disciples planned to take JESUS to this village on a Good Friday. They traveled by bus in a torrential downpour. Suddenly the bus lurched as two tires blew. They ground to a halt. Then a fire broke out, and the disciples had to escape the bus through the windows.

As they stood under a tree, an attempt to be sheltered from the heavy rain, lightning struck an electric power pole a short distance from them. They turned to

Team members carrying film equipment

see what happened only to jump when a second lightning bolt thwacked a nearby tree. This was turning into more of an adventure than they anticipated.

A second bus lumbered down the road and stopped to pick up the drenched travelers and their baggage. When they reached the end of the road, the disciples hoisted the film equipment on their shoulders and set off on a trail up a mountain. When they came to a river swollen by the downpour, they held the equipment above their heads as they waded through the waist-deep torrent.

Finally the weary evangelists arrived at the remote village where the people worshiped dolls. They prepared to show JESUS as the rain stopped. Six hundred people watched JESUS that night, the first time they had ever heard about Him. Two hundred eighteen made a decision to follow Christ.

Then JESUS traveled to a small village in Malawi where the inhabitants shielded themselves from the gospel by their strict adherence to ancestral worship. Using secret rituals, men in masks danced in a way that they believed would allow the living and the dead to interact.

The disciples expected resistance from the village chief, so they were surprised when he readily granted permission to show JESUS. The disciples prayed as the villagers gathered, asking God to break the power of darkness. The people watched JESUS attentively, and many people confessed their need of a Savior.

In response to the film, the village chief said, "Our eyes have seen new things." The next day the disciples led the first discipleship class at the chief's own house with many people in attendance. The group agreed to meet every Sunday afternoon for Bible study. The light had come to this village.

Later, while JESUS traveled in Tanzania, he came upon a clan that claimed their god lived on a certain mountain. They believed a man could not go to that mountain and live unless he was chosen. However, one member of the clan could not justify this teaching with the fact that he saw Christians go to the mountain and return without experiencing harm.

Then JESUS came to the area. This man could not openly attend the showing, so he secretly slipped in. When he watched Jesus being crucified, tears filled his eyes with grief. He felt a weight had been lifted off his shoulders as he acknowledged Jesus died for his sin. He slipped out as soon as the film ended.

Later this man found the disciples to tell them what had happened within him. They affirmed the work that God had done in his heart. He asked the disciples to pray that his clan would see the transformation in his life and give him permission to share JESUS with them.

After that, the disciples took JESUS to Southeast Asia. There they met a man who lived his whole life in a small settlement of a mountainous region. Villagers respected the man because of his devotion to their religion and his ability to perform signs and wonders as part of their religious practices. As animists, the people of the village believed that spirits inhabited everything: rocks, trees, insects, people.

The man strongly protested when JESUS arrived. They did not need a competing religion, he argued. They had their own beliefs that should not be disturbed. The disciples prevailed and received permission for a series of showings. In spite of his protests, one night the man quietly slipped in to watch JESUS. He was moved by the suffering Jesus endured even though He was without sin. Unable to contain himself, the man shouted, "Jesus, have mercy on me. I am a sinner." That same night three others made a decision for Christ, bringing to 18 the number of believers in that small village.

ATHEISTS BELIEVE

When JESUS visited a particular region in Africa, he met a man whose life had been volatile. The community in which he lived as a boy promoted ancestral worship. Believing that the spirits of departed family members stayed near the village, the people offered sacrifices to their ancestors. Sometimes they would dance themselves into an ecstatic state so the spirits would possess them. This man, however, walked away from the traditional beliefs of his family.

As an adult he became an official in the Marxist government and followed the party line of atheism. He did not believe that God existed. In his capacity with the government he frequently persecuted the followers of Jesus. Many people suffered because of his actions.

He lost his position and influence when the government collapsed. The new leaders arrested former officials, and he spent time in prison. He began to ask himself questions while confined. *Who am I? Where did I come from? Why am I here? What will be my end?* He did not find the answers he sought.

When released from prison, the man moved to a part of the country where people did not know about his past. He wanted to make a new start, but the questions continued to haunt him.

He became very ill. Since the medical care he needed was not available in that area, the man moved again. His condition worsened.

Then one Easter he met JESUS, and the transformation started. He marveled at God's love. He found answers to the questions that had plagued him for years. Four days after first seeing JESUS, the man made a decision for Christ. A great peace filled his heart, and he found meaning and purpose. He rejoiced in God's goodness in spite of his great physical needs.

At the urging of his pastor, he had an AIDS test. It confirmed the dreaded disease. But this new Christian does not fear death because he has seen the resurrected Lord.

❊　❊　❊

Once a devout man invited the disciples to bring JESUS to his community in Argentina. Many professional people lived there. While the disciples considered the request, they didn't expect much of a response from the comfortable, self-sufficient families who resided there. However, the man insisted that his neighbors needed Jesus, so the disciples made arrangements for the showing.

At first people appeared a little standoffish. They watched JESUS from their homes, sitting on their front porches. Gradually, though, they came closer to get a better view. About 80 people ended up at the showing that night.

Two women sat together, each drinking a soda as they watched JESUS. They asked which political party sponsored the event and the purpose of the gathering. The disciples responded that they did not represent any political party. They just wanted the people of the neighborhood to meet Jesus. When one of the women heard the name "Jesus," she quickly announced that she was an atheist, but she stayed to watch JESUS in spite of her disbelief.

When the disciples gave the invitation at the end of the film, this woman was one of the first to respond. After seeing JESUS, she abandoned her unbelief in God as she confessed her need of a Savior.

JESUS then traveled to Uruguay. The disciples set up the screen in front of a house occupied by an elderly couple. This couple had spurned everything associated with organized religion. For 86 years the husband would have nothing to do with the church. He considered himself an atheist. Now the church had come to his front yard.

On the night they showed JESUS, the man sat on his patio and watched. He made no response that night, but the seeds of the gospel had been planted.

A few days after the showing, his wife had a heart attack. When her recovery allowed her to return home, the man called the pastor of the local Nazarene church to request a visit. As the pastor talked with this couple, faith began to remove blocks of unbelief and resentment that, over the years, had constructed what seemed like an insurmountable barrier. It took some time and several visits, but eventually this couple confessed their sin in prayer. The encounter with JESUS transformed their lives.

EYES TO SEE

One day the disciples heard a woman shouting in a village in Southeast Asia. They thought the woman might be in childbirth, so they went to investigate. Instead of a mother-to-be, they found a demon-possessed woman. A shaman (witch doctor) stood over her, trying to placate the demon. The disciples did not feel they should speak at that moment, so they prayed silently that God would open the eyes of the people to the truth.

About that time a man in the crowd recognized them. He had met the disciples when they brought JESUS to other towns in the region. He told the disciples about a sick man in his family and asked that they visit to pray for him. The disciples went to see the sick man, eager for an opportunity to minister in Jesus' name.

When they walked into the house where he lay, they found sadness on each face. The shamans had given up on this man, telling him he would die soon. The disciples, in contrast, spoke words of hope as they told the family about Jesus. The whole family believed in the Savior.

God answered the prayer of the disciples that day. God did open the eyes of people to the truth.

JESUS and the disciples then went into the desert. Not many people visited this Kenyan village because of its desolate location. When the disciples arrived, everyone in the village, both young and old, eagerly wanted to see JESUS. The fact that the people heard Jesus speak in their native dialect made a deep impression on them.

After seeing JESUS several times, one woman wanted to testify to what happened to her. "I never heard about Jesus before. When I go home from these meetings I am a happy person. My frustration and anger are gone."

This woman and her family are now followers of Jesus and members of the church.

Then JESUS went to Zambia to speak to the Tonga people. The village leaders warmly welcomed the disciples. That evening they showed JESUS to several thousand people, too many to get a precise count.

The 99-year-old headman responded with great passion. "I did not know that Jesus was a Tonga when He was on earth many years ago," the elder stated. Then he began to weep as he told about his wife's death just eight months prior. "She did not have the chance to meet Jesus," he cried.

The other headmen requested the disciples take

42

JESUS to other villages in the region. They said, "There are hundreds of graves in our villages filled with the bodies of those who did not know Jesus, and that makes us sad. Please come, and maybe our children will choose to accept Jesus." People in this Tonga village knew that Jesus was the Messiah, the Anointed One of God.

"The people were delighted with all the wonderful things [Jesus] was doing" (Luke 13:17b).

FOUR

The Cross Walk

Town after town, torrents of people flowed toward Jesus, the man they had heard so much about. By the time thousands had gathered, people endured quite a bit of pushing and shoving. Some lay trampled by the surge of the throng.

On occasion the crowds seemed much too large, like the time Jesus' mother and brothers stopped by to talk with Him. Since the crowd kept them at bay, they passed a message through a human telegraph line. They told a person near them, who told the next person, then the next, and the next until the message got to Jesus.

The disciples grew weary of the crowds. One time Jesus and the disciples tried to get away for a little rest. When someone spotted where they had gone, the word spread quickly and people came running. Jesus welcomed them, though, cheerfully talking to them about the kingdom of God. As the shadows lengthened in the late afternoon, the disciples wanted to send the people away to find food. Jesus ordered the disciples to take care of the meal, but because of their fatigue, the disciples could not see any options. So Jesus took what was available—five loaves and two fish—and blessed it. When everyone had eaten their fill, several baskets of morsels remained.

Jesus used every opportunity when people gathered to teach them. Sometimes the crowd would sit as Jesus taught. On other occasions the lessons were part of the conversation as they walked down the road.

Once while Jesus traveled with His disciples, He made some very startling statements. Discipleship, He said, required a total commitment. Neither a person's immediate nor extended family could come between a person and God. In fact, Jesus said, the person must give up his or her very self for the sake of the Kingdom. Then, as if to put the final punctuation on His words, Jesus said that discipleship consisted of nothing more or less than a Cross walk.

"Anyone who does not carry his cross and follow me cannot be my disciple" (Luke 14:27).

COURAGE DURING INTIMIDATION

JESUS went with a disciple into a very dangerous region. While on this journey the disciple hired a shoeshine boy to polish his shoes. A rebel approached, angry that the boy would serve someone before him. The rebel shot the boy in the head, splattering the disciple with the boy's blood. Another time the disciple sat

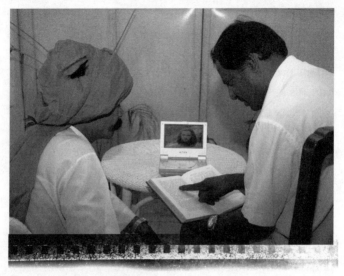

The gospel is secretly presented to a Muslim.

with others in the back of a cargo truck. Rebels demanded money in exchange for protection. When the extortion attempt failed, the rebels sprayed the truck with machine gun fire. Bullets hit the passenger next to the disciple, wounding him in the leg.

During his trip the disciple showed JESUS to one person at a time, always in secret. In three months of very dangerous ministry, the man introduced six Muslims to Jesus. In spite of the risk, he eagerly planned to return to the region because many people expressed interest in seeing JESUS.

In another dangerous area, a disciple worked diligently to share JESUS with friends in his community. He always worked quietly with one person at a time. Over several weeks, however, it became evident to community leaders that he was a Christian. Three men training to be Muslim leaders confronted him and commanded that he cease evangelizing. A long conversation ensued in which the disciple clearly introduced Jesus to the three antagonists. One man made a decision for Christ on the spot. The other two ran from the house in fear. Church leaders baptized the new believer, and he joined the underground church in that city.

Several disciples took JESUS to a village in east Africa. They encountered a great deal of resistance since militant Muslims controlled the area. The disciples sought permission for a public showing of JESUS, but the government officer in charge hesitated to issue them the letter of approval. For 30 minutes the disciples pleaded their case. Finally the leader consented. With the letter in hand, the disciples prepared to show JESUS.

They faced disappointment when only about 20 people came to the first showing. No one came close but stood off at a distance—near enough to see JESUS, but not so close as to be identified with the showing. At one point the disciples stopped the film and urged the people to gather in, but no one did, so they just continued with people standing on the periphery. At the end of the film the disciples issued an invitation to make a decision for Christ. No one responded. A bit discouraged, the disciples simply announced the location of the guest house where they would spend the night. The disciples packed up the equipment and went to their lodging.

About 10:30 P.M. a worker from the guest house knocked on their door to tell the disciples they had visitors. When they ventured into the night, they were surprised to find 15 people who wanted to talk about JESUS. In subdued tones, the night visitors lobbed question after question to the evangelists. They responded with answers about Jesus, the Savior of all. Their answers satisfied the visitors.

"We could not come forward after we saw JESUS because we were afraid of being punished," the visitors finally confided, "but we want to follow Jesus." With whispers in the dark, the disciples led their new friends in a prayer of confession. The family of God increased that night because disciples faced intimidation with faith. When the disciples left a few days later, 40 believers gathered for a worship service before their departure.

DEATH THREATS

Disciples from Lima, Peru, went to a suburb to help the local Nazarene church introduce JESUS to people in the community. The neighborhood had a well-deserved reputation for violence, but the disciples chose to share the gospel in spite of their safety concerns.

A large crowd gathered to see JESUS. Ten minutes into the showing, two men slipped up behind two disciples. Knives gently poked the surprised victims who instantly knew the weapons were capable of much more. No one else at the showing realized that robbers moved in their midst.

Under the cloak of darkness, one of the thieves went for the equipment cases. In the process he stumbled into the projector, causing it to fall to the ground. Now everyone knew something was up. The robbers fled in the commotion.

With the robbers gone, the disciples went to the fallen 16mm film projector. When they set it upright, they saw that the arms which held both the film and take-up reels had snapped. It looked like they would have to send the people home without seeing JESUS. They prayed for guidance then came up with a new plan. The projector would feed the film past the lamp and lens; the problem was with the reels. So a disciple supported one arm and another disciple held the other. A third disciple kept winding the film onto the take-up reel. They did this through four reels of the JESUS film. Sixteen people met Jesus that night.

The intoxicated man pulled the trigger. Nothing happened. The disciple stood unharmed.

* * *

A young disciple in Argentina made arrangements to take JESUS to a community near Buenos Aires. A drunken man decided to halt the showing. As he staggered into the place where they were meeting, he fired his shotgun into the air as a warning. Then at point-blank range, he shoved the gun at the disciple who thought he had spent his last day on this earth.

The intoxicated man pulled the trigger. Several witnesses heard the trigger mechanism click. Nothing happened. The disciple stood unharmed.

The drunkard wandered off as JESUS continued speaking. Later, men from the community took the shotgun from the man. They found it loaded and fully functional. God protected His servant that day.

JESUS continued traveling through the countryside, sharing the Good News. At the end of the year, the district assembly delegates rejoiced in the report: over 1,000 new members since the last assembly, almost a 20 percent increase. But the victory was not without sacrifice. One pastor died in rebel crossfire. Another pastor was murdered after showing JESUS in a rural area. Three other disciples were killed in separate incidents after working with JESUS. All these deaths occurred in one year. But the darkness could not extinguish the Light of Christ, and the Church grew.

ROCKY SOIL

After showing JESUS one night, the disciples visited with members of the community the next day.

That's when they met Selvaraj. Five years prior he had been a leader of a gang that terrorized Christians. Evangelists who came to the village had to get past the formidable barrier Selvaraj and his cronies put in their paths.

But Selvaraj suffered a spinal injury that left him unable to sit or stand or walk. As he lay in his bed, the disciples talked to him about Jesus. This time he listened to the Good News instead of shouting down the messengers. The Sunday after the home visit, two of his friends used a bicycle as a makeshift wheelchair to help Selvaraj attend the worship service. The Christians prayed that Selvaraj would make a decision to follow Jesus, the Savior he once attacked so voraciously.

Then JESUS went to a neighborhood in Ecuador where a gang of delinquent youth often terrorized. Four people had recently died from gang violence, including two related to church members.

In spite of the risks, the congregation planned to share JESUS with their neighbors. The disciples prayed and fasted, asking God to embolden them and empower their efforts. During one of these prayer meetings, the gang burst into the church building and demanded that they stop assembling. The gang members left as soon as their message had been delivered. Undeterred, the people simply continued praying.

The night arrived when JESUS came to the neighborhood. People began to venture out of their houses and congregate near the film equipment. The disciples noticed that the leader of the gang slipped into the crowd too. They monitored his actions as he watched JESUS. During the invitation they were surprised to see him quietly repeat the sinner's prayer. Tears ran down his cheek, which he quickly wiped away. As soon as the film stopped, he ran into the darkness.

Two days later this young man showed up in the neighborhood. People watched him cautiously as he purchased a soft drink. He noticed the apprehension. "You no longer have to be afraid of me," he announced. "I have given up my weapons and destructive lifestyle. I'm a new person." The people could see the tremendous difference in his behavior.

As he said good-bye, he added, "I'll be seeing you. May God bless you."

They found his body two weeks later. The word on the street was that his old gang murdered him because of his decision for Christ.

* * *

JESUS went to the rugged mountains of Southeast Asia. This created quite a challenge for the disciples because sometimes they had to lug the equipment up 6,000 feet of steep terrain.

Stiff opposition formed another obstacle. Villagers beat the disciples when they first took JESUS to one village. Even the two young girls among the disciples suffered physical abuse. But they kept going to the village, and soon a small but solid group of Christians emerged

Carrying the *JESUS* film through the mountains

from their efforts. That success strengthened their resolve. They courageously planned larger, more public events where JESUS could be shared.

When the disciples organized the first Church of the Nazarene in this country with 20 charter members, the second congregation was almost ready to be organized. Four more preaching points showed promise. These church plants in rocky soil took root because of the faithful ministry of disciples in difficult circumstances. First one team, then two, and ultimately five evangelistic teams worked in this arid spiritual climate.

People in one particular village invited the disciples to bring JESUS. When the disciples arrived, they saw everyone working in the fields. They left their baggage on the trail, went into the fields, and worked alongside the local families. When the chores were done, they all sat down to watch JESUS.

The faithful ministry in this country paid off. Two years later they had more than 60 people ready for baptism. When the day for the baptisms arrived, all involved faced two concerns. Because of political unrest, the baptism had to occur before the evening curfew took effect. And then there was the rain. A torrential downpour kept them waiting three hours. When the storm passed by, the sun came out and the Christians walked down to the river for what may have been the largest baptismal service in this nation's history.

In less than four years, in spite of extremely difficult conditions, the church had grown to 14 fully organized congregations with about 700 members, 13 church-type missions with about 300 associate members, and 57 preaching points with another 1,000 adherents. JESUS had come to this country, and the disciples eagerly took up the Cross walk with Jesus.

"After this, Jesus traveled about from one town and village to another, proclaiming the good news of the kingdom of God" (Luke 8:1).

FIVE

Healed and Delivered

When even Jesus' mother and brothers couldn't get close to Him because of the crowds, Jesus suggested to His disciples that they go across the Sea of Galilee in search of solitude. A storm came up while they sailed, one that frightened even the most experienced sailors among them. Jesus was so tired that He slept through the storm. The physical exertion of constantly serving needy people required He get some rest.

When they arrived on the eastern banks of the lake, a demon-possessed man came running up to Jesus just as He stepped out of the boat. This troubled man lived in a graveyard and constantly tore at his clothes until he was naked most of the time. When Jesus saw the man, Jesus commanded the demon to come out of him. The demon barked back, "What do you want with me, Jesus, Son of the Most High God? I beg you, don't torture me!" (Luke 8:28b). The demon did not want to endure torment like he brought to the man.

The dialogue continued until Jesus learned that many demons possessed this man. Jesus permitted them to leave and enter a large herd of pigs on a nearby hill. The pigs stampeded, throwing themselves off the cliff into the lake. Those responsible for the pigs ran into town to spread the news. The townsfolk hurried to find the troubled man now at peace and sitting calmly with Jesus. Terrified by the deliverance, they demanded Jesus leave the area.

When Jesus returned to the west side of the Sea of Galilee, the crowd soon located Him. They had searched for Him and felt glad to be with Jesus again. While on His way to the house of Jairus whose daughter was gravely ill, Jesus suddenly stopped and demanded to know who touched Him.

Those nearest to Jesus looked at each other, confused by the question. No one had touched Him in the way His question implied.

"Peter said, 'Master, the people are crowding and pressing against you.'

"But Jesus said, 'Someone touched me; I know that power has gone out from me'" (Luke 8:45b-46).

Until that moment no one had noticed the woman behind Jesus. Trembling, she came forward and fell at Jesus' feet. She explained how she had been bleeding for 12 years. No one could help her. But she truly believed that if she could just touch Jesus' robe, He would heal her.

Jesus gazed at the woman's face for a moment, then said, "Daughter, your faith has healed you. Go in peace" (Luke 8:48b).

TRANSFORMED BY THE HEALER

Mani lay in bed, the pain from the leprosy making it almost impossible to move. For more than four years the open sores brought suffering. Social isolation too. His wife, unable to handle the distress, left him . . . alone.

Then the disciples found Mani and introduced him to JESUS. Mani accepted Jesus as his Savior. The disciples visited him every week to pray and study the Bible together. They applied ointment to his sores and cared for his physical needs. In a short time Mani stood up and walked. Soon his wounds healed completely. Mani praised God for the healing touch on his body.

After this JESUS went to a town where a man named Maximo lived. Maximo was just 38 years old when an accident paralyzed him. A rock fell on him, and he injured his back. After four years of lying in bed and having others care for him, Maximo decided to kill himself. His wife discovered the poison he intended to drink. She took it away from him and begged him to see JESUS.

Friends took him in a wheelchair to JESUS. As Maximo watched Jesus heal the sick, he wanted to be healed too. The disciples gathered around Maximo to pray. They rejoiced when it became evident God had answered their prayer. Maximo walked again. Now he tells others what Jesus did for him.

In another town, Kusum lay ill with a sickness that

progressively worsened. His fever made him delirious, and his family worried he had gone mad. They did not have the option of seeing a medical doctor, so they called a sorcerer to treat Kusum. No improvement.

About this time JESUS came to their town. Several family members saw JESUS and asked the disciples to visit Kusum. The disciples knelt beside him and asked for God's healing. Jesus touched Kusum and completely took away his illness. Kusum is now a disciple too.

On another day JESUS went to the slum where Trupti lived. Just 18 years old, Trupti had been sick for most of her life. Her father worked as a day laborer; her mother cleaned houses. A significant portion of their meager earnings went to buy medicine for Trupti. She and her parents, plus two sisters and a brother, lived in a shantytown because of their low income and high medical expenses.

Then JESUS came to visit. Trupti felt at peace as she learned about Jesus. She read from the Bible and reflected on the extent of Jesus' suffering. Her own pain seemed minor in comparison.

The disciples prayed for Trupti, and God miraculously healed her.

POWER OVER EVIL

When JESUS went to Tanzania one September day a witch doctor attended the meeting. He watched as a large number of people committed themselves to Christ. This displeased him because he knew that his business would diminish in the same proportion as membership of the church increased.

While the disciples prayed with the people who came forward to accept Jesus as their Savior, a large snake slithered into the gathering.

> The witch doctor came forward and confessed. In an effort to disrupt the meeting, he had used evil powers to send in the snake.

Frightened by the snake, many people ran away. Others took sticks and began to beat it. This enraged the snake, and it escalated its menacing actions. Finally one of the disciples shouted, "I command you to leave in the name of Jesus!" The snake stopped moving . . . dead.

As the commotion subsided and people began returning to the meeting area, the witch doctor came forward and said he had something to confess. In an effort to disrupt the meeting, he had used evil powers to send in the snake. Instead of evil being victorious, however, he saw that the power of God overwhelmed his attempts. The man asked for forgiveness.

Later, people gathered in another area of Tanzania to see JESUS. A noticeable shiver went through the crowd when they saw a 70-year-old woman join those who had assembled. The people feared the woman because of her anger and violent actions.

When the woman saw JESUS drive demons from the young boy, she started shouting. No one could control her as she moved toward the screen. "I want to be set free from the demons," she cried. The crowd sat stunned as the woman continued. "I have killed three boys and one girl in this village. The demons keep demanding more blood. I don't want to kill again."

Jesus met the woman that night. She gave her life to Christ.

* * *

JESUS traveled through Malawi. Ragged stems of maize stalks and weeds covered the field in which the people gathered to see Him. After watching Jesus heal the sick, several women asked the disciples to pray for their children. The disciples reported that evil spirits came out of the children.

Two young men had watched the disciples pray for the children. Finally they walked to the front and asked to speak. They acknowledged they started working as sorcerers while still young boys, having been taught witchcraft by their grandparents. "We have killed many people through witchcraft," one man confessed, "both young and old. We ask Jesus to forgive us and give us a new heart."

The disciples counseled them that only through the blood of Jesus could they be cleansed and freed from the bondage of sin. The young men recognized the truth of the gospel, repented of their sin, and accepted Jesus as their Savior and Lord. They became part of a group of 18 believers who formed a new congregation.

The disciples then went to a place near the Malawi

Children eagerly watch the film.

and Zambia border so people could see JESUS. Many people attended the meeting. They expressed great sorrow as they watched Jesus mocked and sentenced to death. Their lament turned to confession as a good number responded to the invitation to make a decision for Christ.

An 11-year-old girl approached a disciple. She wanted to know if Jesus could cast out Vimbuza, the local name for demons. The girl had been tormented for years. She could not attend school because of the demon that possessed her.

Her parents had tried in vain to find freedom for their daughter. They took her to witch doctors who organized Vimbuza dances. Late at night, accompanied by drumming and clanging metal belts, the dancers intensified the frenzy until they entered a trance. They believe that through the trance they can gratify the spirits enough to lift the curse and bring healing. For severe cases, the dance may end with an animal sacrifice at dawn. No effort like this had freed the girl from the stranglehold of the demon.

The disciples asked to meet the girl's parents the following day. The parents warmly welcomed the disciples and listened intently as they heard about Jesus. When asked if they would like to meet Jesus, the little girl and her parents eagerly expressed their desire to know God. They confessed their sin and asked Jesus to be their Savior.

Then the disciples prayed specifically that the demon would be banished from the little girl. That day it was as if Jesus spoke, "Little girl, your faith has healed you. Go in peace."

"At that very time Jesus cured many who had diseases, sicknesses and evil spirits, and gave sight to many who were blind" (Luke 7:21).

SIX

Wailing to Rejoicing

Simon heard the crowd before he saw it. The wailing, the sorry sound of wailing. Who can describe the cry of women in distress? The volume of the sound suggested a rather large crowd.

As the people came into view, he noticed the Roman soldiers goading a Man carrying a wooden crossbar. Simon stepped into the street to get a better look. The Man labored to take step after step. A ring of thorny vines encircled His head like a crown. Drips of blood ran down His face where a thorn pierced the skin. His robe, soiled, torn, looked like He had repeatedly fallen to the ground.

A soldier grabbed Simon, pushed him toward the Man, and forced him to take the crossbeam. He felt the heaviness of the wood pinch a nerve in his shoulder. Simon adjusted his load as he stumbled down the street behind the condemned Man. His own robe frayed where the wood fibers clawed the fabric. Once fairly clean, the robe quickly collected grime, smudges of drying blood, sweat.

When they reached the place of execution, the crowd watched the gruesome deed. The religious leaders sneered at Jesus with curled lips. The soldiers mocked Him. The vinegar they gave Him only intensified His thirst. One of the criminals being executed fired insults toward Him.

The cacophony reached a crescendo. Then, "Jesus called out with a loud voice, 'Father, into your hands I commit my spirit'" (Luke 23:46a). Bewildered, suddenly subdued, the crowd looked on as Jesus took one more breath, then died.

The centurion who commanded the soldiers surprised everyone when he began to praise God. He did not gloat because of his obvious power. Instead, he marveled at the remarkable Man who had just died. He recognized the potency of righteousness and gave God praise.

The crowd that followed Jesus through the streets, and the women who wailed at the horror, now beat their chests in anguish. Their grief, too great for vocabulary and syntax, found expression in moans and flailing. This Man who had healed their children and commanded demons into the abyss now hung limply on the Cross.

His closest friends, "including the women who had followed him from Galilee, stood at a distance, watching these things" (Luke 23:49b).

POWER OF THE CROSS

Very few disciples lived in this region, in part

because of the repression of the political establishment and the superstition of the citizens. As the doors of the country began to open, however, more and more people expressed an interest in knowing about Christ. When a group of people met the disciples in one town, the inquirers insisted they see JESUS. They were not prepared for what they saw.

Four women sobbed at the shock of the Crucifixion. As they watched Jesus scream in pain, they wept uncontrollably. They instinctively recoiled with each hammer blow as the soldiers drove spikes through Jesus' flesh.

How could this be? Jesus healed the sick. Jesus offered hope to the marginalized. Jesus did not deserve maltreatment.

In a neighboring country, a small group gathered to see JESUS. One man began weeping as he watched the Roman soldiers crucify Christ. No one else seemed moved like this man. Some of the others asked him why he cried. "I felt sorry as I watched them drive the nails through Jesus' hands and feet," the man explained.

His response caused the atmosphere in the room to change dramatically. The shuffling ceased. No one spoke. They watched in silence as Jesus died.

❊   ❊   ❊

A witch doctor in Kenya did not want JESUS in his village. He joined the crowd, intent on disruption. He attempted to compel the forces of evil to halt the proceedings. He uttered curse after curse to no avail. Faced with complete failure, he decided to hang around to see JESUS.

As the witch doctor watched Jesus being crucified, he let out a startling scream. He fell to the ground, belly to the dirt. "Please forgive me," he cried. "Please forgive me."

The disciples hurried to him. There, facedown on the ground, the man confessed his sin and asked God to forgive him. He accepted Jesus as his Savior. The great sacrifice that Jesus paid convicted the man of his sin and provided new life. The following day, the former witch doctor invited the disciples into his home as he began new life as a follower of Jesus.

Empowered with a divine boldness, the disciples asked village leaders for permission to show JESUS. For years the village had been known as a place where Christians were harassed. The village leaders hesitated. They didn't want anything to disturb the peace. Finally they decided to allow JESUS to come. They added a disclaimer to their permission: "We will not take responsibility if people beat you and destroy your equipment."

The disciples recognized the great risk, so they prayed for safety and guidance. Sensing that God had heard their prayers, they chose a central location for the showing.

A gang of young men began making plans to disrupt the disciples. They had a reputation for ambushing travelers on the roads leading into the village and demanding money in exchange for safe passage. If the travelers did not pay the extortion, they jeopardized their very lives. The gang leader also worked as a hit man for other criminals in the region.

Members of the gang slipped into position as JESUS started, awaiting the cue from the leader to attack. When the gang leader saw the Crucifixion, however, he signaled that the operation was off. Nothing in his experience had prepared him to hear Jesus say, "Father, forgive them."

"Is there a person in this world who forgives the persecutor?" he wondered.

The gang leader met Jesus that night. The transformation was dramatic and immediate. Instead of driving them out of town, he helped the disciples find a place to stay. He urged them to show JESUS to other villagers in the region, offering to accompany them for their safety. They could use him as a reference if anyone threatened them. He talked with his friends, urging them to leave their criminal ways and follow Christ.

The disciples then took JESUS to a prison in Uruguay. The inmates began to cry as they saw the Crucifixion. They covered their heads in shame when they realized their sins nailed Jesus to the Cross.

Pablo, of cell 59, met Jesus in that prison. "I cannot forget the face of the little Baby in Mary's arms," Pablo said. "I cannot forget the screams of pain as the nails pierced His hands. I am amazed that Jesus died

A newly organized Nazarene church

for me. Actually, I feel dirty. Jesus should not have died. It should have been me because I'm the sinner, not Him." Even though Pablo continues to serve a 10-year sentence, he lives free in Christ.

After that showing, the disciples began to contact the prisoners' families. They started a house church for the families of incarcerated men. When people in the neighborhood heard the disciples had visited inmates, they were surprised. People avoid prison, they thought, not deliberately visit the place. As more and more neighbors met JESUS, it became necessary to find a place for worship. One of the new Christians gave the church a piece of property on which to build a house of worship.

The changes to the inmates amazed the warden. Because of the encounters with Jesus, the prison was transformed. The authorities opened other sections of the prison to JESUS: the infirmary where the sick and wounded lived and death row where the condemned waited. Opportunities opened to visit other prisons. The national television station heard about the revival and broadcast a feature story. The disciples lifted high the Cross to proclaim Jesus is Lord.

ALIVE IN THE LORD

On another day people packed a church building. With someone in every seat, the children sat on the floor across the front of the sanctuary with others sitting in the aisles. Several rows of people stood in the back, negotiating sight lines so everyone could see JESUS.

Many in the room had never heard the story of Jesus before, so they had no idea how the narrative unfolded. Sobs and gasps sounded from every part of the room as the people watched the soldiers whip Jesus. The people began to feel the torment Jesus endured and the terror the disciples experienced. The shock of what they saw eventually choked back all sound until a potent hush enveloped them.

The emotional intensity increased until the moment Jesus died. A sense of utter despair filled the room. Unable to endure the heavy atmosphere any longer, a young boy shouted, "Don't be afraid. I saw it before. He gets up!"

✳ ✳ ✳

An elderly man in Africa watched JESUS for the first time. The Resurrection amazed him. "In the Koran," he said, "we read that Jesus did not die but was taken to heaven by the power of Allah. But today I saw the way Jesus rose from the dead."

The man asked a disciple to tell him who gave Jesus power over death. When the man learned that God raised Jesus from the dead, he acknowledged Him as the only true God. "If Jesus has really risen from the dead, as I have learned, He is more than a mere prophet." Yes, my friend, Jesus is God.

In another area of Africa, the disciples seemed surprised to see 15 Muslims respond to the invitation to learn more about Jesus. Five of them confessed their need for a Savior. One man was so thoroughly transformed that he boldly testified to his new faith. Threats would not dissuade him. "We will not wait and see our people go to hell as they serve a dead Mohammed," he declared. "We will tell our brothers who are still in the mosque about Jesus."

One African woman went into labor during the showing but refused to leave. About the time of Jesus' resurrection, the woman delivered twins.

One African woman had never experienced "cinema" before seeing JESUS. She went into labor during the showing but refused to leave because of the wonder of the moment. About the time of Jesus' resurrection, the woman delivered twins. Babies born. Mother born again.

In another part of the world, Joona continued the idol worship his family had passed down from generation to generation. He also practiced magic where he would dupe those who came to him for spiritual guidance. He made money by cheating the people. But Joona did not have peace in his heart. His family suffered because of poverty and illness.

Then JESUS came to Joona. As he watched, Joona noticed the miracles Jesus performed. At first he thought it was just magic, but when Jesus died then lived again, he began to comprehend the power of God. He said that the Resurrection "particularly affected my heart. I learned that without Jesus I cannot know life."

Joona denounced idol worship. He abandoned the magic. He is alive in the Lord.

Later, more than 300 people crammed into a house church to watch JESUS. The animated crowd interacted with the film throughout the entire showing. They cheered when Jesus performed a miracle. They laughed when He put the Pharisees in their place. They wept as they watched Jesus whipped and nailed to the Cross. The greatest response, however, was yet to be heard. When Jesus rose from the grave a mighty roar filled the house. Over 100 people accepted the Risen Lord as their Savior that night.

"It is true! The Lord has risen" (Luke 24:34*b*).

Transformed Lives

What a humorous sight! Here was a wealthy, sophisticated man running down the street like a little boy. He desperately wanted to see Jesus, but the crowd blocked his view. So he hurried to get in front of the crowd. To give himself an added advantage, especially since he was short, Zacchaeus shinnied up the trunk and climbed onto the low branches of a sycamore tree. Perched like a boy waiting for a parade, he had a prime lookout from which he could get a clear view of Jesus as He walked by.

But Jesus did not walk by. Instead Jesus walked right up to the tree, called Zacchaeus by name, and told him to come down immediately.

How did Jesus know his name? Zacchaeus knew *about* Jesus but had never officially been introduced.

Then Jesus added, "I must stay at your house today" (Luke 19:5b).

Why the imperative? Why did Jesus speak with such urgency?

The splendid idea of a houseguest, however, overpowered all questions. Zacchaeus immediately hopped out of the tree and walked with Jesus to his house where he gladly welcomed his new Friend. They almost looked like two boys on the way home from school.

The crowd that followed Jesus began to grumble about the unexpected encounter. They despised Zacchaeus and his kind. He collected taxes. The local tax authorities were notorious for gathering more than the Roman government required and lining their pockets with the excess. As the head of all tax collectors in the region, Zacchaeus epitomized everything that people hated about the system. The people could not understand why Jesus would socialize with someone as despicable as Zacchaeus.

In the middle of the meal, Zacchaeus stood to address Jesus. "Look, Lord! Here and now I give half of my possessions to the poor" (Luke 19:8a).

This was no small commitment. Jericho prospered during this time. The tax receipts were plentiful and so was the cut Zacchaeus pocketed. To give away half of his wealth showed a generosity not expected of tax collectors.

Zacchaeus continued, "And if I have cheated anybody out of anything, I will pay back four times the amount" (Luke 19:8b).

No one expected restitution from a tax collector either. Something wonderful had occurred for Zacchaeus to act so out of character.

"Jesus said to him, 'Today salvation has come to this house, because this man, too, is a son of Abraham. For the Son of Man came to seek and to save what was lost'" (Luke 19:9-10).

A NEW CREATION

Joao sold sandwiches on the streets in Brazil. To his advantage, JESUS came to the street where Joao set up his stand. The crowd that gathered to see JESUS quickly purchased Joao's supply of sandwiches. Instead of leaving like he usually did after selling out, Joao stayed to watch JESUS. Since many people had gathered in the street, he had trouble seeing, so Joao

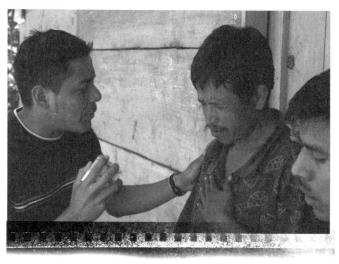

A man accepts Jesus as his Savior.

climbed on top of his car. When the disciples invited people to make a decision for Christ, Joao came down from the car. Jesus went home with Joao that day.

Later JESUS went to a Brazilian beach. A man named Luciano also came to the beach that day. He wore a dark cloak, not what a person would expect as beach attire. The people who lived in the neighborhood looked cautiously toward Luciano as they gathered to see JESUS. One woman said to a disciple, "See that man sitting on the bench, the one in the dark cloak? He's a drug dealer." Instead of keeping his distance, like those who knew Luciano were doing, the disciple went over to introduce himself.

After the conversation, Luciano remained on the bench to watch JESUS. At the close of the film Luciano responded to the invitation. As the disciple counseled him, Luciano confessed that he sold cocaine and crack. He pulled back the dark cloak to reveal the gun he carried. "I can never leave my house without my gun," he said. "Do you guarantee that nothing will happen to me if I accept Jesus as my Savior?" The disciple assured Luciano that the Christians would not do anything to threaten him.

In the days following, the disciple maintained contact with Luciano. During the first visit, the disciple invited him to attend a home Bible study. Luciano agreed. When the disciple, his wife, and two children went to get Luciano, he wanted to clear up something before he went with them. "I have my gun," he stated.

"If you can really guarantee that nothing will happen to me, I will leave my gun in the house and go with you. Think about your answer because if something happens I will kill you, your wife, and your children."

The disciple quickly asked God for protection. He looked at his family, then turned to Luciano. "You can leave your gun in the house." Luciano followed the disciple's instructions. For the first time in years, Luciano left his house unarmed.

When they returned to Luciano's house after the Bible study, Luciano asked the disciple to wait at the car. He went into his house and returned minutes later carrying several items: marijuana, cigarettes, cocaine, and the gun. He handed these things to the disciple and announced, "I don't need them anymore. I have Jesus."

Luciano's faith would be tested in the weeks ahead. Luciano ran into some drug dealers who threatened to kill him. He acknowledged they had the power to do so. Then he testified that if they did, he would die peacefully. "You can kill the body," he testified, "but you can't kill my soul. My soul belongs to the Lord Jesus Christ."

The drug dealers looked at Luciano in disbelief. "Are you a Christian?"

"Yes," Luciano responded, "I am a Christian."

In another region, Kafatiya created quite a reputation for himself. Everyone in his village in Malawi knew him as a thief. He stole crops and chickens and goats.

He took household items, anything of value that he could sell to get a little money. Kafatiya had been convicted, sent to prison, then released, only to repeat the routine again and again.

The vicious cycle came to a screeching halt the day Kafatiya met Jesus. Something dynamic happened when he confessed his sins and repented of his evil ways. To those who had gathered to see JESUS, Kafatiya publicly pledged never to steal again. "I am a new man," he testified.

Kafatiya didn't stop with the one public confession, however. He returned to his home area to tell others what Jesus had done for him. The people could hardly believe what they heard. Many others started attending church because of Kafatiya's testimony in both words and deeds.

In Kenya, residents of a small village suffered as a result of several violent skirmishes. Sometimes innocent bystanders died. When the disciples took JESUS to the village one week after the recent bloodshed, they found security very tight. The authorities insisted they operate within strict guidelines.

A businessman came to see JESUS. His son was one of those killed the week before. When the disciples invited people to receive Jesus as their Savior, this man responded. As he testified later, the man talked about the grief he felt. Those who listened wept as he described the pain of his loss. Then he pointed to Jesus as an example of someone who did not seek revenge for those who mistreated Him. The man closed by asking the people to pray that he would be able to forgive the ones who killed his son. God had begun a deep work in his heart.

NEW HEART, NEW SPIRIT

Diego painted his bedroom black. Spiders and bats adorned the room. Dark drapes hung over the windows to block the light. Only 18 years old, Diego was deeply involved in satanic worship. He treated any adult with disrespect and often offended his neighbors.

Instead of being totally repulsed by his antisocial behavior, one neighbor began praying for Diego. Challenged by church leaders in Ecuador to make a list of 10 people who needed to meet Jesus, then pray for them, the disciple put Diego on her list.

She invited Diego to come to a meeting to see JESUS. Not interested in seeing the film, Diego thought he might meet some girls, so he accepted the invitation. Diego's encounter with Jesus that night changed him completely.

The morning after he met Jesus, Diego started learning what it means to be a disciple of Christ. He joined the disciples who took JESUS to neighborhoods and towns. He eventually became the leader of a prayer group that met in his neighborhood.

The most visible change in Diego's life, however, could be seen in his bedroom. He opened the windows to let the sun shine in. He painted the room a light color. He swept out the spiders and bats. His mother noticed the dramatic change in her son. Three months later, she, too, made a decision for Christ. God had penetrated the darkness with glorious light.

✻ ✻ ✻

Faustin wanted to kill. His uncle had sold the family's house in a major city of Côte d'Ivoire and returned to his home village. When the new owner came to take possession of the home, none of the family members knew anything about the sale. The new owner, fearing the loss of his investment, would not allow the family time to contact their uncle to resolve the crisis. They had to leave the premises immediately.

That made Faustin angry, very angry. As he walked the streets of the city, now a homeless man, he plotted revenge. He would attack the new owner. He would kill him.

As Faustin trudged and plotted, he came upon a group of disciples. He stopped to see JESUS. He listened with great interest as Jesus said, "Love your enemies. Do good." Faustin felt like JESUS spoke directly to him.

Faustin returned to see JESUS the next night. This time as he watched the Crucifixion, he felt sorry for the great injustice Jesus experienced. Faustin identified with Jesus on a very deep level. He made a decision that night to follow Christ and gave up all plans for revenge.

Then JESUS traveled to another community where He met an eight-year-old Fijian boy. When the disciples went to the boy's home, they found the family in turmoil.

The boy's father did not have peace. In spite of being a leading Hindu priest on their island, he lived in a state of despair. To provide for the family, the father had a business where he sold items used in Hindu worship.

The disciples had gone to the house to teach the son, but they soon began to counsel the father. They told the father about Jesus. They talked about hope, about the Prince of Peace.

The father considered their words carefully. To choose Christ would mean he would reject Hinduism. He would lose his identity as a high-ranking priest in the community. He would give up the source of the family's income. The cost would be great.

But he also considered the bondage in which he and his family lived. When he realized the cost did not compare with the great freedom Jesus provided, he asked Jesus to be his Lord. The transformation began at once.

The man immediately rid his house of all remnants of his former religious life. He used a sledge hammer to destroy that which would not burn. He set fire to that which would. By the end of the day, all traces of the old were gone. The new had come.

The man had a concern greater than a clean house, however. He bore the responsibility for inviting an evil spirit to possess his 17-year-old daughter. She recently had run away from home. When he discovered where she had gone, he used the last of his money—a great sacrifice now that he did not have a business to support the family—to hire drivers to take him, his wife, and the disciples to find her.

They found a mess when they walked into the house where the girl had been staying. The room looked as if a typhoon had blown through. The place was in shambles. The girl bit her arms, intent on harming herself.

The disciples began to pray. The girl's mother cried. Her father paced the floor.

The demon in the girl began to talk. In a deep voice with a chilling tone, in a slow, strained pace, the voice that sounded like a huge man came out of the twisted lips of a teenage girl. "You have no authority to send me away," the demon moaned. "I have nowhere else to go."

One of the disciples knew from his own experience about the powers of darkness. And he knew how to respond to the demon.

The disciple crouched in front of the girl. He looked directly into her eyes even though she diverted her gaze. "Don't look away!" the disciple spoke directly to the demon. "Look me in the eyes. I have the authority bought by the blood of Jesus Christ, the Son of God. You are not welcome in this girl anymore!"

The girl writhed with violent convulsions. The struggle continued for some time as the demon resisted the command of the disciple. Finally, the demon left.

The girl's parents and the disciples witnessed the most incredible transformation they had ever seen. The girl relaxed. Peace came to her face. For the first time she looked the disciple in the eyes. She started to weep. Her mother wept, too, only this time they were tears of joy. Her father stopped pacing and started praising God.

The Sunday before the girl had been possessed by a demon. Now she stood liberated because of Jesus.

Three days later the whole family attended the Sunday worship service. For the first time in their lives they walked into a Christian church. The Sunday before the girl had been possessed by a demon. Now she stood liberated because of Jesus. The Sunday before her father had served as a Hindu priest. Now he served the one true God. The Sunday before the family had been in turmoil. Now the whole family rested in the grace and peace of Christ. An encounter with JESUS had transformed their lives.

"All the people were amazed and said to each other, 'What is this teaching? With authority and power he gives orders to evil spirits and they come out!' And the news about him spread throughout the surrounding area" (Luke 4:36-37).

EPILOGUE

From January 1998 through October 10, 2006, JESUS Film Harvest Partners evangelistic teams have reported 41,158,853 evangelistic contacts, 7,168,826 decisions for Christ, and 2,230,433 initial discipleship follow-ups. This has resulted in 9,953 new mission churches and 14,230 new pastors in training. The Church of the Nazarene is currently using 190 *JESUS* film language translations in 99 countries.

"Now to him who is able to do immeasurably more than all we ask or imagine, according to his power that is at work within us, to him be glory in the church and in Christ Jesus throughout all generations, for ever and ever! Amen" (Eph. 3:20-21).

CALL TO ACTION

After reading this book, please consider doing one or more of the following:

1. Go to <www.jfhp.org> for additional stories about the *JESUS* film ministry in the Church of the Nazarene. You will also find special reports, news releases, and discipleship resources at this web site.

2. Request the JESUS Film Harvest Partners weekly "Prayer and Praise" newsletter by sending your E-mail address to <prayers@jfhp.org>. Or you may sign up at <www.jfhp.com/prayer/signup.cfm>.

3. Explore ways you might use the *JESUS* film where you live. See <www.thejesusvideo.com/strategy.htm> for 16 ideas on how the *JESUS* film can be used in the United States and Canada.

4. Use "Window to the World," the curriculum created to teach the English language using the *JESUS* film. See <www.jesusfilm.org/resources/window/index.html>.

5. Pray for the *JESUS* film team members, especially those who show the film to one person at a time in very dangerous situations.

6. Organize a *JESUS* film ministry trip to purchase and deliver film equipment to a team in another country. Contact the JESUS Film Harvest Partners office at (913) 768-6500 x100 or by E-mailing info@JFHP.org for more information, or see <www.jfhp.com/getinvolved/trips.html>.

PRONUNCIATION GUIDE

The following information will assist in pronouncing some unfamiliar words in this book. The suggested pronunciations, though not always precise, are close approximations of the way the terms are pronounced.

Akbar	AHK-bahr
Bako	BAH-koh
Côte d'Ivoire	KOHT Dee-VWAHR
Faustin	foh-STE
Hortensia	hohr-TEN-see-ah
Joao	jew-OU
Joona	JEW-nah
Josiane	joh-see-AN
Kafatiya	kah-fah-TEE-yah
Kamanga	kah-MAHNG-gah
Kusum	KEW-suhm
Lima	LEE-mah
Luciano	lew-see-AH-noh
Mani	MAH-nee
Maximo	MAK-see-moh
Raj	RAHZH
Selvaraj	SEL-vaw-rahzh
Trupti	TREWP-tee
Vimbuza	vim-BEW-zah
Yohana	yoh-HAH-nah